Rust, Shadow, Dream

Rust, Shadow, Dream

Poems by

Ann Sheils

Kelsay Books

© 2018 Ann Sheils. All rights reserved. This material may not be reproduced in any form, published, reprinted, recorded, performed, broadcast, rewritten or redistributed without the explicit permission of Ann Sheils. All such actions are strictly prohibited by law.

Cover photograph: Ann E. Sheils

ISBN: 13-978-1-947465-28-2

Kelsay Books
Aldrich Press
www.kelsaybooks.com

*Dedicated to Kay, Lucy and Andrew—
gifts that I am in no way deserving of*

Acknowledgments

The Wayfarer: "After Thoreau"
In the Perennial Garden, Finishing Line Press: "Et in Arcadia Ego"
Time of Singing: "Pilate's Wife"
In the Perennial Garden, Finishing Line Press: "The Stream"
Main Street Rag: "Hike"

Contents

Rafted Up	13
Aubade	14
Hurricane	15
The Apple	19
Soon	21
Surprise	22
Hammersmith, 1973	23
Pilate's Wife	25
Loss	26
The Stream	27
Remembering the Hills	29
The Leash	30
November 2001	31
To a Lizard	32
Before Freon	33
Hysterectomy	34
Hike	35
Antique Shop	36
Nativity	37
Departure	38
Et In Arcadia Ego	39
Battle	41
Gone	42
After Thoreau	43
Morning Song	44
Line Squall	45
Pentecost	46
Phoenix	47
Recital, St. John's	48
The List	49
Weeds	50
Outside the Budding Grove	51
The Craft	53

About the Author

"We must regard man as little more than a chance deposit on the surface of the world, carelessly thrown up between two ice ages by the same forces that rust iron and ripen corn...."

    Carl L. Becker, *The Heavenly City of the Eighteenth-Century Philosophers*

"For man walketh in a vain shadow, and disquieteth himself in vain; he heapeth up riches, and cannot tell who shall gather them."

    Psalm xxxix, from "The Order for the Burial of the Dead," Common Prayer

"...We are such stuff as dreams are made on, and our little life is rounded with a sleep...."

    Shakespeare, *The Tempest*

Rafted Up

Wind and tide contend in Penton Island Sound,
where Chatham River meets the sea.
We bounce in chop,
barely able to pass our drinks and canapés,
neighbors on the nearby bluff
for thirty years or so,
and could be thought an ad for luxury
in later middle age.

Four boats have sidled up to one another,
anchors set, bumpers arranged.
Gusts blow words from group to group—
this season's tulips, admired in Amsterdam,
tented parties, hunts in Argentina.

Beneath this comfortable accounting
lurk quieter talks, invoking other days:
a daughter still in hospice care,
a failing business, murdered uncle,
malignancy and heart disease.

Our cocktails float on fragile fiberglass
this perfect April evening,
but waiting in dark water under us,
ready to devour,
swims all that we would forget.

Aubade

The impediments to longer sleep
are a tumult of birds
announcing worms or mates,
and the further river clamor
of clanking halyards, straining hinges.

Magnolia and gardenia
drift through opened windows,
from a lawn where fig and orange trees
also find the sun,
between shady stands of mossy oaks.

From my bedside radio
an airline pilot describes
ghastly miles of smoke,
spied almost from the stars,
along the burning Amazon,

and underneath his cockpit,
rafts of undecaying trash,
twice as large as Texas,
that wheel in empty oceans
home to only jellyfish.

Fetid seas will come here too,
where fewer shrimp and crabs,
burdened by undigested plastic,
find our nets and baskets,
where a torn primordial aquifer
salts our bodies and the land,
while drought withers
a once wet corner of the earth.

Hurricane

I

A small god
on my gleaming steed,
I am making dirt.
Thor has his hammer,
Apollo has his bow,
I have mulching blades
to create a rich amalgam
for my realm.

Out at sea the Big God
has imprinted the water
with the whorls of his thumbprint,
so that my subject trees
may soon drop limbs
large as compact cars,
shed branches
long as Christmas trees.

Stories recount how in such ways
giants fought with gods,
lesser deities battled greater ones,
who obliterated paltry kingdoms
with vigorous breath.

II

My fragile imperious mother
will not evacuate.
Her still nimble brain
leaps ahead of all my arguments
and those of every fraught official,

until the thought of no AC
motivates the truant widow,
though this old city
hasn't had a catastrophic storm
for at least one hundred years.

We survive the exodus and eventual return,
complicated by beauracractic schemes,
to find that God has laughed.
I feared enormous trees
that despite careful pruning
overhang our country bedroom
like the sword of Damocles.
She feared a hot city home
whose windows are nailed shut,
subsequent to several burglaries.

My roof remained intact.
but her home was hit from the lane,
by a massive pecan tree
we didn't even know was there,
while uncommon weather kept her house
cool beyond imagining.

Now the town lies torn and crumpled
under tattered trees.
Glowing in a gentle evening sky
of baby pink and blue
that tourists would photograph
if they were here,
an emoticon moon
looks down upon us all,
smiling its silly grin.

III

I don't ignore the grief and tragedy
of lost life, and damaged homes,
but the gardener in me
mourns the rows of trees,
whose corpses line the streets.
The young ones like infant death—
all those cells dividing, all the straining veins,
all that budding and stretching,
lifeless in a mound--
while the majestic old, too large to move,
lie where they are fallen,
generals, having seen much life
stir beneath them,
finally surrendered, after violent contest.

IV

I could almost shoot sea gulls,
massing on dock rails,
gossipy congregants in pews,
harshly squawking,
perhaps about recent scavenging.
Miniature white vultures,
carnivores that peck at whales when surfacing
and foul my dock as soon as I scrub piles
of sloppy excrement.

But this mew stands alone
on an oyster rake,
observing the tide wash in,
seeming to ponder his circumstances.

His wing droops,
torn in the hurricane,
and my pity is aroused.
He examines his resources,
abandoned by mobbing cohorts,
then pushes off into the river,
a small white craft
listing to one side.

The Apple

The Apple is, always.
We were made
for not knowing,
for eternally hoping
to discern the Word
from outside the lost garden;
for parsing the story,
which if it isn't true,
should be.

Without the work
of grasping shifting shadows
of proclaimed certainty,
we--who wrench truths
with forceps,
or deliver them
after long labor,
with the sweet tug
given a slippery infant--
would not be.

There is a chaste Beloved,
whose fingers
we can only brush,
whose descriptions
by the holy men
leave us haunted
by a missing climax.

Knowing,
we need no faith,
and gossamer hope
becomes leaden certainty.

Soon

it will be too late to leave these walls,
the halls' turns known without reckoning,
where I do not stumble
on familiar Persian knots,
nor fail to find the bed,
the pillow plumped by hands
that once plumped me,
the coverlet worn thin
by the fierce darling dog,
who sighed in gratitude
against my leg for twenty years.

This house and land
are my old paint pony,
who stumbles to the barn
when I have dropped the reins,
the conveyors of memories
that return without urging,
and allow me to know who I am.

Surprise

The raft noses the shore.
A dull circle of leaves opens
and kaleidoscopes to the sky,
a rabble of iridescent color
and psychedelic pattern.
The butterflies' round unfolding
is heaven's vessel,
a hieroglyph of God.

Many dozens hover there,
like a rapturous chord
lingering in still air.
Staggered by such magic,
I exclaim to the others.
The crusty guide replies,
"Those are only black winged swallow tails.
Someone must have peed.
They love urine."

Hammersmith, 1973

I

Because he wears turquoise pants with red socks,
along the river promenade,
there is no romance.

And because three old women
sit alone at separate tables
in the café at teatime,
while new leaves lick the window
on this first spring day;

And because the mother slaps her child,
and the brittle-faced boy
throws his cigarette from the car,
and violent music slashes through willow trees
from the Georgian window;

And because the elegantly limbed young man
doesn't ask me to sail with him
when I admire his boat,
and because when I finally invade the pub, alone,
timidity overcome by the flush and press inside,
by the bouquet of ale and liquor
from the open door,
the air and talk and faces are stale.

There is no romance
because I pace round and round the post box
and cannot write you, simply, purely, "Come."

II

I do not wheel a pram
in Ravenscourt Park,
so the ecstasy of solitude
on this crystal day,
luminous with every shade of spring,
is shattered.

I should be poised high above,
a red balloon, slick and bright
as tulips here below.
Instead I am a puppet
whose strings
are the stares of men,
rudely focused,
like cameras of tourists.

Pilate's Wife

She knew,
without parables or prophecies,
dusty years given the disciples;
without stilled seas, loaded nets,
injunctions at the well,
or broken bodies healed
to foretell restored humanity.

At the beginning was
the instant joy of Elizabeth,
and Anna's instant thanks.
At the end,
she likewise knew at once,
with the certainty
of that group of futile women,
not of her kin, or creed, or state,
Daughters of Jerusalem silenced
by the men who swayed her husband,
yet who weeping followed
the scarlet robe and thorns,
forewarned by Him
of babies roasted by the famished,
of bodies split
in search of swallowed treasure,
of fig and olive groves
cut for a thousand crucifixion timbers
in the years that were to follow.

Loss

I

It was almost enough,
almost enough, he thought,
to admire her long thigh's taut curve,
under the prim skirt or slacks,
at their random and chaste encounters.
And once, while helping with her coat,
he had brushed the weightless hair
from the nape of her white neck.
There were clumsy hugs at greeting and goodbye,
that sometimes relaxed enough for him to know
how well her body folded into his.
Does she know, he asked, does she ache
for what time and circumstance
have denied?

II

One day he was bold enough to say
how good she looked in brown.
He might have thought
that rarest hues would complement her best,
the intimate flush of a seashell's depth,
the silvered underside of an aspen leaf,
the magenta of a winter dawn.
But it was the quiet brown of a nested wren,
an autumn field lying down for winter,
or the morning mocha he stared at deep in thought
that brought her to him.

The Stream

The friction of the southeast trades
urges surface water into small verticals,
while the earth's spin
seizes the slanted spray
and flings it westward,
until disgorged from the swollen Gulf,
it pours back to the Atlantic.

Others blithely cross this jewel stream,
but above the diesels' roar
and the slash of twin propellers
through its six knot flow,
so wide and deep its volume equals
a thousand Mississippis,
I hear Pip's demented cry.

On this crossing
I learn about a recent castaway,
who, bound for Bimini,
fell from the gleaming fiberglass,
his screams masked by sea-slap
and the engines' throb.

Did terror first come
with the blue-sailed man-o-war,
or with the shark's insistent bumps
against his dangling legs,
helpless as an infant's?
Did he gape at starfish
in the inverted heaven
stretching godlessly beneath him?
And did he rage like Pip,

like all appalled by loneliness,
at the resolute backs
turned away?

Remembering the Hills

Here at the frontier's ragged edge,
distance is misunderstood
without reference—barn, ranch house,
something to scale these bald monstrosities--
or an eye that enlarges to discover
that the tempting lapis lake
folded into blue-black conifers
is dark and deep and cold,
under a sky saturated by day,
in unrelieved blue,
like a child's finger paints,
without nuance or gradation,
and at night becomes a jeweler's box
opened to frozen glitter.

I remember lustrous hills,
and homes in their green embrace,
the long days of a single season
swathing fences with vines too thick to cut,
until, under the round bowl of yellow stars,
darkness gathers, and all the lush subsides.

The Leash

You hated the leash,
all eighteen pounds
straining against it,
somehow pulling me
up the mountain trail.
Released, you ran five miles
for each one I walked,
fighting marmots, chipmunks, and porcupines,
disappearing too long into muddy bogs,
skulking back to find me angry and relieved.

Now, with gray temples
like an aging leading man's,
you still bear a lithe and muscled body
proudly around the town,
and tolerate the leash.
It means that I am close,
seeing and hearing for you,
guarding you from thunder,
and the angry hiss of air brakes
on giant trucks,
as we walk sidewalks,
instead of wilderness.

November 2001

A boon, because
at the garden center,
on this golden afternoon,
they must unload the trees,
too early for taste or faith.

So I peruse perennials,
still lush with summer blooms
at half their price,
while Christmas tunes
recalling bleak mid-winter
seep through the humid air.

Across the street, tires squeal,
and then a thud.
People gasp and run.
A fearful glance reveals
a large white dog
much too still.

Back home, I plant and prune,
shadowed by tragedy and doom,
because that thud has echoed
since September,
in the heart of every mother,
after bodies met the earth
in unimagined ways.

To a Lizard

Four spatulate feet
cling to my white Suburban
with the might of your few ounces,
conveyed down Truman Parkway
at speeds impossible
for the lizard brain to know.
If I stopped the motion
of the universe you clutch,
in a seeming act of mercy,
you'd be another stain
on greasy macadam.

Your slit eyes discover me,
a presence dark behind the glass,
but cannot know my hope
that you survive
this hot and wind-torn passage,
from asphalt parking lot
to the green lawn
that you were made for,
sweet and lush
beyond reptile imagining.

Before Freon

heat lay too heavy
for anything but shelling beans
under the screened porch fan,
our thumbs bruised and green
from splitting firm skins
beyond the sun's long reach.

Then, windows opened
to raucous calls of jaybirds in the oaks,
scolding squirrels as we awoke,
and to shrill insistent cries
of women in the street
singing, "yea crab, oyster buy,"
pungent baskets balanced high
on salt-stained, turbaned heads.

In the lane staccato hooves
brought milk in sweating bottles
from the dairy near the train,
where our class was sent to practice
evacuation in the rain,
the year that Cuba threatened.

Shedding heat in the roiling surf
we'd see who rode waves farthest,
whose belly scraped the worst.
There was not much cold but melon,
or hand-churned peach ice cream,
on the porch where breezes bore
the sea oats restless clatter,
and the nearby ocean's roar.

Hysterectomy

No more scouting conveniences,
no more intervals
proscribed by the moon,
enforced abstinence,
or spectral conceptions.
Uncomplicated as a man—
will I become as simple?

Hike

Gasping from absent air,
I see death in peaks ahead
instead of splendor;
fear the arduous return
to tapestried meadows below.

Fast food burgers, lapsed discipline,
and squandered hours
make me stumble up a stony trail
with an ominous thumping heart,
in a painful climb
that could have been a dance.

Antique Shop

I can't resist the other lives
tumbled next to one another here,
where air rains dust of the dead.
A vanquished Rebel's bust
gazes at Nazi guns,
Okie tools rust on Cracker wagon wheels.
Mid century formica abuts walnut
carved by Chippendale.

On the wall,
in tarnished silver frames,
prints of roses
joust with new geometries.
Among these remains,
who am I today?

Nativity

for Jane

A dozen moons have glowed over this home
since I last unwound each figure
from its nest of tissue.
Soon a doctor's call will tell us
whether I or someone else
will unpack the box next year,
for the dear celebration,
in these sere and darkening days,
of the Word and the womb,
and the consequent empty tomb.

Under the chipped wings of angels
the Virgin kneels,
obedience has breaking the iron chain to old death.
Shepherds gather
in witness to an ancient promise
fulfilled beyond their yearning.
The Magi arrive
at the shining they have sought,
where imagination loses its shadowed places.
The Child sleeps,
haloed by a light
that reveals the world
as it was meant to be,
before time began.

Departure

I'm more relaxed than usual
this summer afternoon,
who often imagines
the plane a fireball,
my dying child alone.
She boards with a quick hug
and I turn to go,
when a nearby man
points to a missing tire,
and says it will delay the flight.

Postponed panic comes,
the absolute need
to feel her hand in mine,
the slight bones
that can propel ecstatic notes
through the long strings
of a concert grand.
But she is gone.

The mechanic surely feels
my impotent maternal watching,
until he shuffles off,
and the plane taxis beyond my view.
Minutes from the airport,
driving home,
rain explodes on the windshield,
lightning skewers a sky
full of sudden thunder,
and I listen for the sound of sirens.

Et In Arcadia Ego

I

After the cyclist died in my husband's arms,
we continued to our destination.
Yet I would never round that curve again
without the image of the Harley overturned,
despite Bruegel having shown us
how easy it is to overlook such tragedy.

Weather, too, acknowledged this victim
more than the Dutchman's Icarus.
We hiked in sun and storm,
a chiaroscuro afternoon
suddenly darkening vivid mountains,
eclipsing neon flowers.

II

After the creek's last turn
we entered the bright river.
Snugged against golden marsh,
boards gliding along black mud,
we had been sheltered from autumn wind
and the scene we glided onto.

Search boats scanned the river
for a man just drowned.
On our thin boards we paddled shallows,
while neighbors peered under docks
and in the beds of oysters for some sign--
an empty sleeve, a boot, a disturbance under water.

He would not be found—
the waters plied all winter
by marine patrol,
our river and our former sport
both haunted by what might be spied
in an embrace of grass or cloak of mud.

Battle

Human heart,
you bloody knot
that can change the great glad world
into a stale drab box,
or that box into a glittering universe,
depending on which devouring twin,
housed in your fist-sized muscle
has had his sway--
whether joy or fear
owns the day.

Gone

He had been married
more than twenty years
before he felt that of all the things
time had impressed upon him,
like a stamp on metal,
his past with her
was not among them.

Ancient Jews must have felt this
when Jesus exorcised the demons,
when they fled bodies at His command,
leaving no trace behind,
not the wet path of a snail,
not the efflorescence
of trailing ocean water.

Now she was gone,
strangely gone,
no ache, no loss,
just the complete present--
work, home, children,
and his beloved wife.

After Thoreau

Even to simplify our shoes
could be a Walden of sorts—
discarding some
pre-Labor Day whites,
or ochre suedes of Fall,
sequinned Santas,
Easter egg pastels,
and the sport specific:
running shoes, boat shoes, golf shoes,
hiking boots and hunting boots—
choosing the simplicity
that poverty begets
or vows require,
an uncluttered closet,
an uncluttered heart.

Morning Song

The last time
we cast for shrimp together,
you were in my womb,
and I ungainly large
for hopping bow to stern
across the mud slick seats.

Now you're old enough
to paddle where I point,
ducking the leaded skirt
when I turn to throw,
and are briefly pleased,
when we glide against the chest high grass,
to spy a raccoon's pointed face
or a heron's beady eye.

Though I tell you of other times,
when one good cast was dinner,
the moon or tide is wrong today,
and you tire of my little chase,
my pleasure just as lost to you
as when you were my small Jonah,
pressed against the heartbeat of the whale.

Line Squall

At the margin of the painting
is massed a colossal silver tower,
the clouds' edges bruised to lavender,
which would be lovely,
except for imagination.

The rendered day is rare:
a cobalt sky and lapis sea
gleam against crisp marsh.
The artist has slapped the water
into stiff peaks,
but not rough enough
to move the small white craft
out of its track toward the sound.

A forecast would be no help—
always the same in summer,
with its omnipresent chance of storms
that can race just east or west of the sailors,
granting them a breezy picnic,
a swim in a sparkling cove,
or find and swallow them
in a black tornadic gale,
like the boating family
dead last summer.

Pentecost

Stage effect tongues of fire
and toppling winds,
ecstatic jabbering—
the stale theatrics of bulletin boards
in countless Sunday Schools,
the subject of urgent signs
on empty country roads.

But then the better drama:
Peter tells of David,
still quiet in his tomb,
that the One seen risen
was assuredly the God-made Christ.

What kind of cry must it have been
from those who had mocked and tortured?
Was there tearing of hair and beards,
a wail reaching heaven,
or the numbed utterance of a pierced heart?

"What shall we do?" is Pentecost,
and the answer,
forceful as flames and babble,
"Change your hearts."

Phoenix

Before fire destroyed
the whitewashed church
and its rusted, blood-red roof,
streaked with black and verdigris,
he had meant to stop and photograph
that small pageant
gleaming in autumn sun.

But young afternoons
propelled him home,
through a limber tunnel of boughs
that swayed with music
ringing from his windows,
to the river,
where in the brief light left,
trout were waiting.

The rebuilt roof is stained again
by half a lifetime's years.
Trees are cut and broken,
trout forgotten.
But the metal gleams
its serendipitous beauty,
offering itself once more,
as he passes by.

Recital, St. John's

First, Haydn in C-major,
singing through the fretted choir,
weaving the invisible
until sound becomes more solid
than carved and gilded surfaces.
Then Mozart's oboe, angel-voiced,
ascending vaulted heights,
ark-like ribs barely able
to contain the sea of sound.

Conjured from the insubstantial--
passion, reverence, madness--
notes float in marvelous abyss
until accumulated into song,
then rise again, re-gathered by another,
the paradigm ecology.

Creation this:
something out of nothing;
no correspondences—
line for leaf, light for love.
God can be if music is.

The List

is too long.
I think of bed,
a pillow on my head
to muffle words
chanting in my brain--
house painting,
floor sanding,
rug cleaning.

Then the storm.
Weeks with a chain saw,
and picking up debris.
Other life recedes--
doctor visits, galas, exercise.

Choices the list, the list life,
vanity or charity,
health or a clean lawn,
saving or damning myself
with each decision.

Weeds

Kneeling in this new garden,
spade in hand,
two thousand miles from home,
I don't know what to kill or keep--
the variety of this wild and varied world
an enigma, a puzzle to be pieced.

Truths, heresies,
clans and tribes do battle,
their roots as tangled
as these unknown weeds and flowers.

Outside the Budding Grove

I never understood
that women were beautiful,
though I was once called that.
Even young and slim
there were a myriad of flaws--
shoulders too broad,
arms dangling like bent saplings,
feet that sweat.

Brotherless,
young males fascinated--
the crew cut boy next door,
whose hair, at once fuzzy and stiff,
I yearned to stroke,
until he peed in the bushes for me.
Older boys played football in the park,
then rolled together in the dirt,
oddly groping one another.
Then came the amorous,
with insistent poker pants,
sprouting wiry hair from soft faces.

 Later, when a young mother,
inextricably knit to only women,
and within the budding grove
of dewy daughters and their friends,
I hardly noticed
the loveliness of girls.

Now pushed from the circle
of young and female
by diminished hormones,

I see with man-like eyes
what I had always missed,
why men turn for even a glimpse
of bare leg, swinging hair, or plump butt.

Over dinner, her bright eyes,
soft mouth and sweet words,
skin un-etched by worry or weather,
show me what I never knew I had.

The Craft

The roofers' rhythmic tapping
on durable slate
mocks my thin cadences,
as they fit heavy pieces
in a precise pattern
composed against the sky.

They laugh in the sun,
supple chests bare,
handing up the proper shape,
nailing without hesitation.
A hundred years from now
these new tiles and gleaming copper gutters
will bear soft moss and subtle verdigris.

Beneath them, pen in hand,
alone on a cold stone bench,
I pause in my austere craft,
watching them secure the final tile,
and clamber down,
free from revision and revision.

About the Author

Ann Sheils lives and writes poetry and fiction in her native Savannah, Georgia. She has had poems published in *The Anglican Theological Review, Dappled Things, Gray's Sporting Journal, Main Street Rag, The Aurorean, The Wayfarer, Time of Singing*, and other journals.

Recently Finishing Line Press published her chapbook, *In the Perennial Garden.*

She has been mentored by Donald Justice at Sewanee Writer's Conference, Ann Hood at Aspen's Summer Words, Tony Morris at Ossabaw Island Writers' Retreat, and Antonya Nelson at the Ah Ha School in Telluride, CO., but initially by The Reverend William H. Ralston.

Formerly a teacher, she now sells real estate. Her leisure time is spent on saltwater, hiking the San Juan Mountains, gardening, golf and tennis. Ann is married and has three adult children.

www.ingramcontent.com/pod-product-compliance
Lightning Source LLC
LaVergne TN
LVHW021625080426
835510LV00019B/2767